The Buzzing Bee

by Holly Harper

illustrated by Liza Lewis

OXFORD
UNIVERSITY PRESS
AUSTRALIA & NEW ZEALAND

Dad and Ella sit on the rug.

Ella gets a jam bun.

4

5

Dad gets in the rocket.

Dad is up high.

I can see the
buzzing bee.

Dad is in a boat.

I can see the buzzing bee.

Dad is soaking wet.